A Listening Season
Sermons for Advent and Christmas

A Listening Season
Sermons for Advent and Christmas

L. Ted Smith

JOHN 1:14

ISBN 978-0-557-72193-1

Contents

Dedication

To Vergie Hatcher Smith, my mother,

from whom I first learned to listen for

the gentle and loving voice of God.

Acknowledgments

This book is the completion of a long-held dream of writing for publication. The old saying is, "The road to hell is paved with good intentions." My good intentions have now become a reality, so I hope that in regard to the matter of writing a book, I am now off the broad path to perdition!

I would like to express gratitude to a number of people who have been a source of inspiration along the way. First and foremost, I am grateful for my wife, Cantey, who has unfailingly supported and encouraged me in the process of writing and who has always been a partner in Christ. She is indeed my soul mate and best friend. My children, Ashley and Ian, have always been kind to their "preacher Dad" about his sermons. I thank them for their support and love and for putting up with being preacher's kids!

I am thankful for Ben Campbell Johnson, my seminary adviser and mentor, who first encouraged me to write and who has been a model for me of both scholarship and gracious Christian witness.

I am deeply grateful for my secretary and colleague in Christian ministry, Becky Ferguson, a called servant of God whose organizational skills and management of the church office has afforded not only me, but all the pastors of First Presbyterian Church of Cartersville, Georgia, for the last forty years, the time to study, to pray, and to write.

I am indebted to the three parishes I have served as a pastor. I thank the good people of Chickamauga and Morton Memorial Presbyterian Churches in northwest Georgia, who allowed me to practice my preaching on them for the three years fresh out of seminary and who taught me so much about being a pastor. The congregation of Peachtree Presbyterian Church in Atlanta provided love, support, and a true laboratory for ministry unlike any other in the Presbyterian Church USA. To them, I say thank you. I must say, however, that I am most deeply indebted and grateful for my current parish, First Presbyterian Church of Cartersville, Georgia. For loving me back to health when I was on the verge of burnout, for renewing and challenging me in ministry each and every day, for giving me the sabbatical time to write this book, and for your constant affirmation, I am thankful beyond words.

Sola Deo Gloria—to God alone be the glory!

Introduction

For nearly a quarter of a century now, I have had the privilege of being a pastor. I am one of those fortunate people who are able to work at a job I love and find deeply fulfilling. It is my hope that I have been effective at my life's vocation. The task that has brought me the greatest joy in ministry is preaching.

St. Augustine in his treatise *On Christian Doctrine* asks, "What is a sermon for?" His answer to the question is that the purpose of a sermon is "to teach, to delight and to persuade." After more than fifty years of life in the church and twenty-five years at the task of researching, writing, and delivering sermons, I can testify to the accuracy of Augustine's definition in my own life. Through sermons—those I have heard as well as preached—I have been taught, delighted, and persuaded in my faith.

In my personal reading, both for spiritual growth and for preparation for Sunday morning, I have benefited from other gifted preachers whose published sermons have greatly informed my faith. Some of those preachers are quoted in my sermons. I hope the mention of their names and their works is a tribute to the Holy Spirit speaking through them to you, just as the Spirit has to me. Hearing the Spirit through others is a sure sign of the truth of that great Christian doctrine we affirm whenever we recite the Apostles' Creed.

Of all the seasons of the year in which I delight in preaching, Advent and Christmas certainly rise to the top. There is something about these seasons that keeps me renewed and inspired in the work of sermonizing. Perhaps it is because Advent marks the beginning of a new church year. Therefore it always seems to bring with it a fresh beginning, a new start. Perhaps it's because Advent usually marks the completion of the annual stewardship campaign, so there are no more "sermons on the amount" for a while! For whatever reason, Advent and Christmas have always reinvigorated me in the pulpit.

Advent, of course, includes the four Sundays before Christmas. The themes of Advent are preparation, waiting, and anticipation of the coming of the Lord. The word *advent* derives from Latin and means "to come; to draw near; to approach." In Advent, Christians acknowledge and prepare for the arrival of Christ. However, Advent doesn't simply look back to the "coming" of Christ long ago as the child Jesus born to Mary and Joseph. Advent also looks forward to the "coming" of Christ—as the king Jesus—again at the end of time. So Advent looks backward as well as forward, to the past and to the future.

Christmas is the culmination of the season of Advent. At Christmas, we acknowledge the presence of the Lord—God's presence that humbly came long ago in the hamlet of Bethlehem with the birth of Jesus, the Son of God. But we also believe that God's presence is a temporary truth—that God in Christ continues to be born anew in us again and again. The joy we experience at Christmas is meant to be a foretaste of the full and final arrival of Christ. Past, present, and future are all caught up together in the celebration that is Christmas.

I hope as you read these sermons you will discern these overriding themes of Advent and Christmas—anticipation, waiting, hope, and joy at the presence of Christ in our lives. As a pathway into these major themes of the season, I propose that we employ a sense we often take for granted, but if applied correctly, can become a spiritual discipline. That sense is listening.

Listening as a spiritual discipline is both counterintuitive and counter cultural in modern times. On the one hand, there has never been a time in human history that is more filled with sound. From iTunes to talk radio, the din is relentless. It seems we listen to so much. Or do we? Are we listening, or are we simply inundated by sound to the point that we, as the prophets of the Old Testament declared, "Hear and hear but do not listen?"

With the cultural celebration of Christmas in America, the spiritual discipline of listening is most certainly counterintuitive. After all, we listen to so much already in this season—Christmas commercials and secular carols. The noise level gets ramped up as we listen to the countdown of the shopping days left until December 25. Even with our best intentions, even in the church, we fill up time and space with programs, events, cantatas, and pageants. To us in the church, these are all very precious moments and a part of our Christian worship during this season. But I wonder sometimes if something deeply and profoundly spiritual gets lost in the holiday shuffle. Intentional listening—creating space where we seek to hear the voice of the living and approaching Christ in this blessed season—may be what we most deeply need.

The Advent sermons I have included in this volume follow the theme of listening. The texts are all Gospel lessons from lectionary cycle C. The texts of Christmas Day and the first Sunday after Christmas 2003 are also from year C of the lectionary. However the sermon I preached the Sunday after Christmas 2006 is the New Year's Day Gospel text for each and every year. That Sunday happened to be on January 2, and it seemed a highly appropriate lesson for the day.

As St. Augustine stated, the purpose of the sermon is "to teach, to delight, and to persuade." If any or all of this happens in your reading of these sermons, I will be both humbled and pleased.

L. Ted Smith

June 2010

Chapter 1

Listening to the World

First Sunday of Advent
2003

There will be signs in the sun, the moon, and the stars, and on the earth distress among nations confused by the roaring of the sea and the waves. People will faint from fear and foreboding of what is coming upon the world, for the powers of the heavens will be shaken. Then they will see "the Son of Man coming in a cloud" with power and great glory. Now when these things begin to take place, stand up and raise your heads, because your redemption is drawing near.

Then he told them a parable: "Look at the fig tree and all the trees; as soon as they sprout leaves, you can see for yourselves and know that summer is already near. So also, when you see these things taking place, you know that the kingdom of God is near. Truly I tell you, this generation will not pass away until all things have taken place. Heaven and earth will pass away, but my words will not pass away. Be on guard so that your hearts are not weighed down with dissipation and drunkenness and the worries of this life, and that day catch you unexpectedly, like a trap. For it will come upon all who live on the face of the whole earth. Be alert at all times, praying that you may have the strength to escape all these things that will take place, and to stand before the Son of Man" (Luke 21:25–36).

It is the Sunday after Thanksgiving, and if all our senses were lost, save for our hearing, we could still tell what season we are in. We could tell by:

- The continuous ringing of the Salvation Army bells in front of Target and Wal-Mart.
- The constant Christmas carols being played on the radio.
- The masses tromping the sidewalks of downtown or the aisles of the mall.
- The increased volume of the retailers' commercials that seems desperate to get us to spend our money in their particular store.

Yes, if we had to, we could tell what season we are in by simply listening. Thankfully, most of us have all five of our senses. We can see the harvest colors and the reds and greens of this time of year. We can smell the cinnamon and nutmeg, the peppermint and evergreen. We can taste the eggnog and the turkey and feel the effects of the tryptophan in that holiday bird making our eyelids heavy.

In one sense, the holiday season is a time of sensory overload. One can perceive so much this time of year that it can almost all meld together into a meaningless experience where it becomes hard for us to distinguish anything of note.

Have you ever felt this way in December, where it is all just too much to take in? I know I have, and maybe you have too. This is where the resources of our faith can help us. Our faith tries to help us become attuned to the sacred in the midst of the ordinary, the holy amid the profane. Our faith beckon us to slow life down enough that we can really see what is happening; to really feel the fullness of life that is being communicated in the biblical message of the season; to really stop and listen to what is happening around us that we might hear the whispers of the divine.

It is stopping and listening that I would hold up as the spiritual discipline for us to consider in this Advent season, this season that we Christians observe as a way to prepare our hearts to receive anew the presence of God that we acknowledge came so decisively in the Christ child born to Mary and Joseph long ago.

I want to challenge you this Advent in the midst of the sensory overload of December to make an intentional effort to stop and listen.

You may at first only hear the same things you always hear in December. But if you give it time and prayer, I believe you will hear the Lord speaking to you in a new and profound way that will allow your Advent and Christmas to be an experience of joy instead of busyness.

And because the spiritual life is a journey into the depths of our own spirits and the spirit of God, I want to suggest that we begin at the most public level in our listening. I want to recommend that we begin by listening to the world around us.

When you listen to the world, what do you hear? I would dare say that you hear something not so pleasant to the ear. The world we live in is a world that exists between advents—between the first coming of the Messiah as Jesus the Child and the second coming of the Messiah as Christ the King. As twentieth-century theologian Karl Barth put it, we live in the "between times." We live in the interim, and in that interim, there is much unanswered and, yes, even much unpleasantness.

Jesus spoke poetically of these "between times" in the passage we read from the Gospel of Luke.

> There will be signs in the sun, the moon and the stars, and on earth distress among the nations confused by the roaring of the sea and the waves. People will faint from fear and foreboding of what is coming upon the world, for the powers of the heavens will be shaken (vv.25–26).

Poetic words, but pertinent to our lives. For when we listen to the world, do we not in fact hear confusion and distress? Don't we hear the fear and foreboding? How could we not? We live in a world where all of these things are a reality.

We are now involved in wars in both Afghanistan and Iraq. But "our" war is just the tip of the iceberg globally in regard to the conflict among nations. In the last twenty years, there have been wars or civil unrest in all of these places: Bolivia, Bosnia, Myanmar, Colombia, East Timor, Indonesia, Haiti, India, Pakistan, Lebanon, Israel, North Korea, Northern Ireland, Liberia, the Philippines, Chechnya, Rwanda, Somalia, Sri Lanka, and the Sudan. And there are probably some I have missed.[i]

Jesus talked about the frightening times that were coming, and we, just like the Christians in Luke's day to whom he wrote, are living in those times, "the between times." If we listen to the world, we cannot help but hear the "fear and foreboding" that Jesus spoke of. Ever since 9/11, we in this country have moved into an "apocalyptic mode," when we are, as philosopher Gunther Anders puts it, "no longer asking ourselves, 'How shall we live?' but asking instead, 'Shall we live?'"[ii]

Indeed, we do face perils in this world. To deny it is to close our eyes and shut our ears. Global warming, the ozone hole, overpopulation, starvation and malnutrition, war, and the AIDS pandemic that has left more than 10 million children orphaned on the continent of Africa. Dangers abound in our world. Can you sense them?

So what am I trying to do here with all this bad news—mess up your holiday spirit? No! I am inviting you to be spiritually mindful of this season. The One whose Advent we celebrate this time of year came into this very world that we are talking about—a world of war, famine, disease, and distress. Jesus, the eternal Son, entered into this world because he loved it enough to experience it at our level, despite all of its "fear and foreboding."

However, as Jesus walked among us, he heard more in the world than the distress; he also heard the world's longing, and it is that to which I turn your attention now. You see, if it were only the "fear and foreboding" that Jesus heard and communicated, he would mean no more to us than any other cultural prophet who knew all of the problems but none of the solutions. But Jesus heard something beneath all the fear and foreboding. He heard human longing as well. It was expressed in the strains of human hope.

The words of Jesus that follow his threatening announcement of the signs of the times are words that I encourage us to focus on in this season, for they are the gospel—the good news—to you and me. For you see, we do indeed live in the time between the advents fraught with difficulty. But we also live on the edge of a hoped-for new world. Jesus, whose spirit was so attuned to God and humanity, heard the longing for a new world. Jesus heard the strains of hope and proclaimed it and embodied it in his life. Listen to his words again in *The Message* translation:

> And then—then!—they'll see the Son of Man welcomed in grand style— a glorious welcome! When all of this starts to happen, up on your feet. Stand tall with your heads high. Help is on the way! (Luke 21:28)

You see, Jesus heard beneath the human reality of fear and anxiety a still deeper reality— the longing for human redemption; and he proclaimed that God was going to respond to that longing. In fact, God already had responded to it in the person of Jesus, the Son of Man.

Today's gospel lesson calls on us to do two things that can be very difficult to do at the same time: to listen to the world's heartache and be realistic about the present; and at the same time, to listen to the world's heart-hunger and not lose hope for the future. [iii]

How do we keep the strains of hope that we hear and that Jesus proclaimed from being drowned out by the cacophony of fear and foreboding? That is the question disciples of Jesus have to address. As we celebrate his first advent while looking forward to his second, how shall we live faithfully? Two things Jesus communicates in this passage seem like good, practical advice for faithful living to keep the strains of hope alive. First of all we can…

…Raise our heads!

The word from Jesus is that when we see all of the disturbing things taking place in the world, we are not to lower our heads in cynical despair but to raise them in hopeful anticipation. In the land of apparent despair, we are to be about the business of cultivating the garden of faith, hope, and expectation. [iv]

There is a scene at the end of the second *Lord of the Rings* movie, when Sam, a hobbit, says to his fellow hobbit, Frodo, "There are things that people hold onto to keep them going." Frodo, who at the time feels like giving up, asks, "What are we holding onto?" Sam replies, "That there is still some good in the world, and that's worth fighting for."

What are we holding onto? We Christians are holding onto hope, for it is one of the "big three" that abide—faith, love, and hope. The apostle Paul once said of hope that "it does not disappoint us" (Rom. 5:5). There is still some good left in this world, and it is that good for which we fight and that good which the living Christ is present in, wherever and whenever that good manifests itself.

And so we "raise our heads." We take our eyes off of ground-level realities, and we look toward the horizon, standing on tiptoe to see what God is bringing us from the future. And it is better than we can imagine. We saw decisive glimpses of it in Jesus when he healed the sick, when he ate with sinners, when he fed the hungry masses, and when he faced the forces of death and injustice on the cross and conquered them in the resurrection. We raise our heads with confidence that God is not through with his creation yet, and one day, as the writer of Revelation says,

> The kingdoms of this world will become the kingdom of our Lord and his Christ and he shall reign forever (). (Revelation 21:20)

So we can "raise our heads." But we can also…

…Raise our self-expectations!

In the 34th verse, Luke recalls these words from Jesus:

> "Be on guard so that your hearts are not weighed down with dissipation and drunkenness and the worries of this life, and that day catch you unexpectedly."

Notice that there are three dangers to advent people who are living between the times— dissipation, drunkenness, and the worries of this life.

The dictionary defines dissipation as "a process in which energy is used or lost without accomplishing useful work." But we don't have to worry about dissipation, do we? We never fritter away our time and energy in our culture, do we? Of course we do! Dissipation is one of the besetting sins of our culture. We expend tremendous amounts of energy accomplishing little in our lives. We fret and worry over where we will spend our next vacation or what our next automobile will be. We fritter away our time and energy as consumers. But are we being useful to God and to our neighbor? If there were ever a season in our social context to consider our spiritual usefulness and whether we are prone to dissipation, Advent is it.

Of course, we all know what drunkenness is, but there are many things we intoxicate our lives with, not just adult beverages. We intoxicate our lives with work, power, ambition, hatred, pleasures, and obsessions.

And how about the "worries of this life?" That could be anything that demands our attention and allegiance more than the Almighty.

Theologian Neal Plantinga hits the nail on the head about all of these when he writes that Jesus is concerned here about the people of God who weigh themselves down with worldly anxieties and then relieve them with world amusements. Or as *The Message* translation puts the thirty-fourth verse:

> But be on your guard. Don't let the sharp edge of your expectation get dulled by parties and drinking and shopping.

Hmm? Sounds a lot like the way most of us Americans celebrate this time of year, doesn't it? By contrast, Jesus bids us to raise our expectations of ourselves, to live as though there is a new world coming.

Lewis Smedes in his book *Standing on the Promises* states:

> "The hardest part for people who believe in the second (advent) of Jesus Christ is in "living the sort of life that makes people say, 'Ah, so that's how people are going to live when righteousness takes over our world.'"

It is that living as though there is a new world coming—living with raised heads and raised self-expectations—that is so difficult to do. But by the grace of God, we can succeed.

And so in this season of Advent, may you listen to the world. Listen to its pain, and join it in its crying. But also listen for its hope, and participate in its anticipation, just as Jesus did, by raising your eyes above the ground-level realities and expecting more of yourself as a follower of the One who loved this world so much that he advent-ed into it as a child and will advent into it again one day as the Son of Man who will set all things right.

Chapter 2

Listening to the Word

Second Sunday of Advent
2003

> In the fifteenth year of the reign of Emperor Tiberius, when Pontius Pilate was governor of Judea, and Herod was ruler of Galilee, and his brother Philip ruler of the region of Ituraea and Trachonitis, and Lysanias ruler of Abilene, during the high priesthood of Annas and Caiaphas, the word of God came to John son of Zechariah in the wilderness. He went into all the region around the Jordan, proclaiming a baptism of repentance for the forgiveness of sins, as it is written in the book of the words of the prophet Isaiah, "The voice of one crying out in the wilderness: 'Prepare the way of the Lord, make his paths straight. Every valley shall be filled, and every mountain and hill shall be made low, and the crooked shall be made straight, and the rough ways made smooth; and all flesh shall see the salvation of God'" (Luke 3:1–6).

In celebration of the season of Advent this year, I am commending to us the spiritual discipline of listening. It is akin to the discipline of prayer—paying attention to God that we might hear God's message to us anew.

The importance of listening is illustrated by a story I recently heard of a four-year-old boy who was visiting his grandparents. He came bounding into his Grandpa's study where his granddad was intently reading. The little boy, named Jason, was carrying a peach and said something to his Grandpa, who, because he was busy reading, didn't catch what the boy said. Jason handed his grandfather the peach.

Thinking his wife had sent him a snack, Grandpa took it and ate it. Just as he swallowed the last bite, Jason, with lip quivering said, "But Papa, I didn't want you to eat it. I just wanted you to get the worm out."[v] Listening can be very important.

In the sermon for the First Sunday of Advent, I suggested that we might begin our Advent spiritual discipline of listening at the most public level—by listening to the world. I recommended that in our listening we follow the pattern of Jesus, who heard two things from the world: its heartache and its hope, and then to respond as Jesus did.

On this second Sunday of Advent, I'd like to challenge you to continue listening to the world, but to also listen to something else—to listen to the word. Of course, the word I'm speaking of is "the word of the Lord." It was a word that was heard that first season of Advent long ago by a man named John, son of Zechariah and Elizabeth. It was heard and heeded by a man whom some call the central figure of Advent, for he came as a forerunner of the Messiah—came to prepare the way for the coming of the Lord. Perhaps what I am hoping is that if we can listen to the word of the Lord as John did, we too might be harbingers and heralds of the coming of the Messiah as Christmas approaches.

The beginning of John's ministry is recorded by all of the gospel writers. However, Luke gives the most detailed description of John the Baptist. Luke's account of John's ministry encompasses most of the third chapter of his Gospel. Consistent with his penchant for history, Luke places John (as well as Jesus) in the historical setting of 28 CE with his opening verses:

> In the fifteenth year of the reign of Emperor Tiberius, when Pontius Pilate was governor of Judea, and Herod was ruler of Galilee, and his brother Philip ruler of the region of Ituraea and Trachonitis, and Lysanias ruler of Abilene, during the high priesthood of Annas and Caiaphas, the word of God came to John son of Zechariah in the wilderness.

Often, we contemporary readers of the Bible are tempted to treat these first two verses as we do the genealogies of the Old Testament—as superfluous to the real story. But they are not simply biblical fluff.

One Lutheran pastor, Leonard Klein says it well:

> If you daydreamed during the first two verses [of Luke 3] you missed the whole point. His point is that everything

> that is about to transpire will occur in history. We know the world in which all this takes place; we are part of it; we can see, understand and believe.[vi]

These first two verses communicate something essential, particularly in regard to listening to the word of the Lord. And it is this: the word of the Lord is spoken into the kind of world that you and I live every day, not a fantasy land of long ago and far away, but this very realm in which we reside.

We could very well translate these verses right into our own contemporary setting, and they would still be the words of scripture:

> In the third year of the presidency of George W. Bush—when Sonny Perdue was governor of the state of Georgia and Zell Miller was a U.S. senator; and Mike Fields was the mayor of Cartersville. When John Paul II was pontiff of the Roman Catholic Church and Cliff Kirkpatrick was Stated Clerk of the PCUSA General Assembly, the word of God came…

What Luke is trying to tell us is that the word for which we listen, the word that was heard and proclaimed by John, comes into this real world—a world where politicians seemingly hold all the power, a world where religious leaders wield authority, the kind of world that we live in to this day. And in this world it is not easy to hear the word of the Lord.

Is it not the case that it is hard to hear God's voice amid the competing voices of rulers and nations? One theologian, Gail Ricciutti, refers to the names mentioned in these first two verses as "reverse witnesses," who have a stake in containing the outbreak of the reign of God.

Here's a chilling story: As he sat in his prison cell in Nuremberg, awaiting his trial for war crimes, Hermann Goering, Hitler's Reich Marshall and head of the Luftwaffe, made the following comment about the sway that government leaders have over their people:

> Of course the people don't want war. But after all, it's the leaders of the country who determine the policy, and it's always a simple matter to drag the people along whether it's a democracy, a dictatorship, or a parliament. Voice or no voice, the people can always be brought to the bidding of the leaders. That is easy. All you have to do is tell them

> they are being attacked, and denounce the pacifists for lack of patriotism, and exposing the country to greater danger.[3vii]

It is indeed hard to hear the word of the Lord over the competing voices in the world. The leaders of the world have an investment in their own kingdoms and do not want to listen to a new word about a new kingdom. How do we hear a word from the Lord when so many other voices cry out? The very culture you and I live in makes it nearly impossible to listen for the word.

Duke University chaplain William Willamon tells about a friend of his who is a pastor in Africa. Upon coming to the United States to visit, Willamon says that he felt so sorry for his friend, for he knew of the lack of resources that he had to operate with in his country. And not only that, but he had actually been thrown in jail numerous times for his evangelistic activity in that politically oppressive nation. As Willamon shared his sympathy for his situation, his friend responded by saying, "I actually have more sympathy for you in America. There is just so much here. You have so much freedom, so many things. What is left to offer people? What needs do they have for which the Gospel could be fulfillment? There is so much, so much fulfillment here, and so little emptiness. The gospel feeds on emptiness.[viii]

And perhaps that is why even though the names of those with power and privilege are mentioned, even though the religious hoi polloi are named, Luke does *not* say that the word of the Lord came to any of them, but that it came rather to a poor nobody prophet called John, son of Zechariah, who was strutting around on the edge of town wearing a camel-hair zoot suit.

But that is the way the word has always been heard: not so much from the thrones of the mighty, but from the chairs and pews of the ordinary men or women who have ears to hear and a heart that is open.

The word of the Lord comes into the kind of world that you and I live in every day, and it comes to the unexpected ones, which means that it could come to you or to me, just as easily (if not more easily!) as it could come to the pope or the president.

But notice the location that John was in when he heard the word from the Lord: he was in the wilderness.

The old saying in real estate is that the three most important things are "location, location, location." Maybe the same is true when it comes to hearing the word of the Lord. Perhaps it is where we situate ourselves that determines how easy it is to hear God's voice. John, we are told, was in the wilderness. Of course, we know that "the wilderness" is a metaphor. It is a metaphor that recalls the wanderings of Israel after the Exodus. In those wanderings, they learned to trust and obey God in new ways. We are reminded that nearly every significant encounter between God and the leaders of the Old Testament was in the wilderness. For it was in the wilderness, far from the trappings of power and privilege, far from the distractions of televisions, game cubes, cell phones, and e-mail, that people could listen for what God was trying to tell them.

Saint Ignatius of Loyola once wrote the following:

> It is true that the voice of God, having once fully penetrated the heart, becomes strong as the tempest and loud as the thunder; but before reaching the heart, it is as weak as a light breath that scarcely agitates the air. It shrinks from noise, and is silent amid the agitation.

When I was a youth, my dad and I would go hunting. One of the things I remember to this day was how my dad listened in the woods. Whether it was when our redbone hound, Lady, was running a rabbit or when we were just sitting quietly under a tree waiting for the squirrels to come out, he always opened his mouth as though he were tasting the sound or taking it into his body. Sometimes the sound would barely agitate the air, but he always heard it.

In the wilderness, John listened for the whisper of God's voice. I can almost imagine him listening with his mouth ajar for that light breath of the Holy Spirit speaking God's word. It was out there, far from the agitation and noise, that John heard the word of the Lord. And it set him on a new path that would forever alter his life.

The message from Luke here for us in our Advent is to carve out that wilderness in the midst of our celebrations. The place where the word of the Lord was heard in this story was not Rome or Jerusalem but the wilderness—that place on the edge of the hubbub. Could it be likely that we will not hear the word of the Lord at Town Center Mall or the Mall of Georgia? Could it be that Toys R Us will not bring us the word we need to hear? There are lots of good movies coming out for the holidays, but we will not hear the word of the Lord at the AMC 24 Theaters.

> And the word of the Lord came to John, the son of Zechariah in the wilderness. (v.2b)

Wherever that place of calm and quiet is—whether it is at home or church or in the car or in the woods—go to that place and listen. Listen! It will be a word of hope that you hear. It will be about the valleys of life being filled and the crooked ways made straight. It will be about the emptiness in the world being replaced with fullness.

But it will also be about changing our lives to make way for that to happen. If you go to the wilderness—wherever that is for you—and listen, be prepared to examine yourself and get ready to change. There is a new world coming, and we must get ready. Our lives, our values, our priorities, and our behaviors must change because the King is coming! And we must be a people prepared.

Having heard the one named John who first heard that Advent word of hope and challenge in the wilderness, St. Augustine leaves us with words to ponder as we continue our Advent pilgrimage:

> He who loves the coming of the Lord is not he who affirms it is far off, nor is it he who says it is near. It is he who, whether it be far or near, awaits it with sincere faith, steadfast hope, and fervent love.

Chapter 3

Listening to the Warning

Third Sunday of Advent
2003

John said to the crowds that came out to be baptized by him, "You brood of vipers! Who warned you to flee from the wrath to come? Bear fruits worthy of repentance. Do not begin to say to yourselves, 'We have Abraham as our ancestor'; for I tell you, God is able from these stones to raise up children to Abraham. Even now the ax is lying at the root of the trees; every tree therefore that does not bear good fruit is cut down and thrown into the fire." And the crowds asked him, "What then should we do?" In reply he said to them, "Whoever has two coats must share with anyone who has none; and whoever has food must do likewise." Even tax collectors came to be baptized, and they asked him, "Teacher, what should we do?" He said to them, "Collect no more than the amount prescribed for you." Soldiers also asked him, "And we, what should we do?" He said to them, "Do not extort money from anyone by threats or false accusation, and be satisfied with your wages."

As the people were filled with expectation, and all were questioning in their hearts concerning John, whether he might be the Messiah, John answered all of them by saying, "I baptize you with water; but one who is more powerful than I is coming; I am not worthy to untie the thong of his sandals. He will baptize you with the Holy Spirit and fire. His winnowing fork is in his hand, to clear his threshing floor and to gather the wheat into his

> granary; but the chaff he will burn with unquenchable fire." So, with many other exhortations, he proclaimed the good news to the people (Luke 3:7–18).

There are some things that are just fun to listen to at Christmas. Don't you just love to hear all the old, popular Christmas carols? What other time of the year can you hear such artists as Bing Crosby, Perry Como, Andy Williams, and Rosemary Clooney on the radio?

Then there is the sound of sleigh bells. You never hear sleigh bells in the South except at Christmas. Or what about the sound of laughter and the excited giggling of children as their expectations grow with the approaching day? There are indeed some sounds at Christmas that are music to our ears.

However, this morning we are asked to listen once again to a sound that we do not enjoy hearing at Christmas. It is the voice of one crying in the wilderness. There are times in Advent that I wish I could go through the season without having to hear John's shrill voice. He does not croon like Bing or Perry. He is not the pretty sight that Rosemary is in the movie *White Christmas*. His message is more foreign to the ear than Andy Williams's melodic intoning. Yes, there are times I wish we could make it through December without having to listen to John the Baptizer.

John is a character who lives with one foot in the world of the Old Testament and one foot in the world of the New Testament. He is a transitional figure, and his message is in keeping with the prophets who went before him. He comes with words that are meant to prepare the way for the coming of the Lord.

In the text from the second Sunday of Advent, we discover that John listened for a word from the Lord out there in the wilderness where he had set up shop, and he heard it. Upon hearing that word, just like the prophets of the Old Testament, it burned with a fiery passion in John's heart, and he had to share that word. But it was not pleasant word. Who would enjoy going to hear some good preaching and being called "a snake in the grass?" That's what the people heard when they went out in the wilderness to listen to John.

"You brood of vipers! Who warned you to flee from the wrath to come?" John lays into people. He is not a pleasing voice to hear in December. Yes, John can truly mess up your Christmas spirit!

But John's is a necessary voice to hear in the season of Advent, for we cannot be fully prepared for the advent of Christ until we have listened to him. And as we listen to the ranting and raving of John, we are bound to hear what I would call…

…A warning jolt!

We already know that tact is not John's strong suit, but telling the truth is. He told the truth that day to the crowds that came out to hear him; John's truth that comes to us across the centuries today is that all is not right with us. We are not ready for the full advent of the Lord into our lives. We are not prepared for God's appearing. We are sinners. We must repent, and we must live out that repentance in our lives.

Repentance means "change." It means an about-face! It means to change direction in life, and that is the truth that John brings us as we prepare ourselves for the coming Lord: to repent, to change, to alter our patterns.

John calls us "a brood of vipers," not to be mean to us, but to jolt us awake to the reality of who we are. We are sinners. We sometimes forget that. We sometimes forget that the first question we respond to at our baptism and profession of faith is "Do you confess yourself to be a sinner in need of God's grace?"

We sometimes forget that. After years of dressing ourselves up for church in our finery, we begin to believe that we are the imaginary person with the coat and tie and the upstanding presence in the community. We start to assume that the person on the surface is who we really are and we can neglect the state of the soul. John jolts us with his warning: Repent! Take no comfort in your old securities! Honestly assess who you are at heart!

Have you ever seen the old movie *The High and the Mighty*? On a flight over the ocean, the pilot's voice announces to the passenger cabin, "We have a problem, and we cannot correct it. We are not going to make it. I tell you this so that you might prepare yourselves for the inevitable."

Upon hearing the announcement, an elegantly dressed woman begins to remove the diamond pendant from around her neck and the large ring from her finger. She peels off her false eyelashes and wipes the makeup from her face. A large scar that the makeup had always concealed is now visible on her forehead. She is preparing herself for the end. She will go there as she really is.

As it turns out, the flight is saved. They make it to the airport, but the woman has changed. Honesty was offered her, and she took it gladly. She removed her mask and became who she really was.[ix]

This is what John offers with his warning jolt: a chance to repent yet again; a chance to face the reality of our lives; a chance to take off the masks; a chance to let go of the things that we think will save us—our church memberships, our good deeds, our jobs, our national power, our technological superiority, our positions, or our portfolios. When we take advantage of the opportunities for change, we can begin to grasp the coming Lord who *can* save. John's warning jolt is not easy to hear in December, but it is essential.

I have to admit that whenever I read what Luke writes about John's preaching in verse eighteen, I get really angry!

> So, with many other exhortations, John proclaimed the good news to the people.

Where's the good news! All I hear is judgment and warning! I am tempted to agree with William Barclay who writes in his commentary that whatever it is that John preaches, it is not good news, not the Gospel.

But the spiritual discipline of listening begs me to reconsider that assessment. Luke called John's teaching good news, and there must be some Gospel in it. If we listen closely and deeply to it, I think we can hear it. The good news in John's warning jolt is this: it can lead us to discover…

…A wondrous joy!

It seems rather strange to read John the Baptist's preaching on the same Sunday that we light the candle of joy in the Advent wreath. I sometimes wonder what the good people who put the lectionary together were thinking when they placed John the Baptist on joy Sunday. But maybe there is a reason. Perhaps the only path to the wondrous joy of Jesus is through John's warning jolt. Perhaps until we see the error of our ways, realize that we need a savior, and admit that we cannot be good on our own, we will never discover the true joy and meaning of Christmas.

John tells us to repent and to bear fruit worthy of repentance. The people ask, "What should we do?" What John tells them is startling in its simplicity:

- Don't hoard, but share what you have.
- Don't cheat people, but deal fairly with them.
- Don't use your power to do harm and hurt, but use your power with integrity to do justice.

Now we know what the path of repentance calls for. What John tells us to do is so simple. But that leads me to a question: Why does it seem we cannot do it? If it is so simple, why do we not do it?

Maybe it is because knowing what to do is only half the battle. We are still left without the resources to fully do what we know we are supposed to do. We need someone to come among us and show us how to live repentant lives. We know the "what," but we do not know the "how." We need someone to model how it is done. John points beyond himself.

> (The) one who is more powerful than I is coming; I am not worthy to untie the thong of his sandals. He will baptize you with the Holy Spirit and fire. His winnowing fork is in his hand, to clear his threshing floor and to gather the wheat into his granary; but the chaff he will burn with unquenchable fire." So, with many other exhortations, he proclaimed the good news to the people

The one to whom John bears witness is mightier than John himself. John told us what to do, but Jesus will show us how to do it. John gives us the warning jolt, but Jesus will lead us to the wondrous joy that comes with lives that can indeed bear fruits worthy of repentance.

"What should we do?" the people ask. John tells the people to *radicalize the love of neighbor in their lives.* But then he points to Jesus who will be the one to model that perfectly. John is saying that the wondrous joy will come in Jesus, who can immerse us not just in water but in the Holy Spirit.

You've heard the warning. You know what to do. Now trust in the One who can show you how to do it, the One who, in fact, did it for us and for all from his cradle to his cross.

The prophet Zephaniah, whom we also hear from in the lectionary on the third Sunday of Advent, foresaw the appearing of this One of wondrous joy, and he give us a testimony as well:

"Rejoice and exult with all your heart,
The Lord has taken away the judgments against you,
The King of Israel, the Lord, is in your midst,
He will rejoice over you in gladness,
He will renew you in his love." (Zephaniah 3:14-17)

Listening to John's warning jolt, we are now ready for the wondrous joy of Jesus. We are ready to let the One who was "born a child, but yet a king" live in us, and we are ready to honestly face who we are. We are ready to let the wondrous joy live in and through us. We are ready for Him to remake us into the kind of people who willingly share, who want to live with integrity and equity, and who want to use our power for good and not for evil.

"The Lord is in our midst," proclaimed the Zephaniah, "exulting over us with joy and love." Let us live worthy of that joy and love as we prepare for Christmas.

Chapter 4

Listening to the Womb

Fourth Sunday of Advent
2003

In the sixth month the angel Gabriel was sent by God to a town in Galilee called Nazareth, to a virgin engaged to a man whose name was Joseph, of the house of David. The virgin's name was Mary. And he came to her and said, "Greetings, favored one! The Lord is with you." But she was much perplexed by his words and pondered what sort of greeting this might be. The angel said to her, "Do not be afraid, Mary, for you have found favor with God. And now, you will conceive in your womb and bear a son, and you will name him Jesus. He will be great, and will be called the Son of the Most High, and the Lord God will give to him the throne of his ancestor David. He will reign over the house of Jacob forever, and of his kingdom there will be no end." Mary said to the angel, "How can this be, since I am a virgin?" The angel said to her, "The Holy Spirit will come upon you, and the power of the Most High will overshadow you; therefore the child to be born will be holy; he will be called Son of God. And now, your relative Elizabeth in her old age has also conceived a son; and this is the sixth month for her who was said to be barren. For nothing will be impossible with God." Then Mary said, "Here am I, the servant of the Lord; let it be with me according to your word." Then the angel departed from her.

In those days Mary set out and went with haste to a Judean town in the hill country, where she entered the

> house of Zechariah and greeted Elizabeth. When Elizabeth heard Mary's greeting, the child leaped in her womb. And Elizabeth was filled with the Holy Spirit and exclaimed with a loud cry, "Blessed are you among women, and blessed is the fruit of your womb. And why has this happened to me that the mother of my Lord comes to me? For as soon as I heard the sound of your greeting, the child in my womb leaped for joy. And blessed is she who believed that there would be a fulfillment of what was spoken to her by the Lord" (Luke 1:26–45).

This Advent season we have pondered the spiritual discipline of listening. It is a most apt season for such a discipline. Julie Johnson, the director of the Spirituality Program at Columbia Theological Seminary, wrote in this month's newsletter:

> In Advent there is so much wonder, mystery and longing. The Living God invites us to pay attention differently during this season. In Advent it's as if there is more spaciousness between the minutes, more beckoning to linger between the hours. Time and space opens to the Holy Brooding One. Time is swirling…and we are invited to wonder, what does God wish to birth in us this year?[x]

Her parting question—What does God wish to birth in us?—is at the heart of this sermon.

As we have considered listening as a means of grace in this season of Advent, we began by listening at the most public level—listening to the world. As we listened at that level, we heard both the world's hurt and its hope. Today we move to the other end of the listening spectrum, and I want to invite you to listen at the most personal level—to listen to what is going on deep within your own being.

I have titled this sermon for the fourth Sunday of Advent, "Listening to the Womb." I chose that title because the womb is literally (and for our purposes, figuratively) the place of gestation and birth. In our scripture today, we have two women, Elizabeth and Mary, and both are in awe of what is happening in their wombs.

Elizabeth's awe is sheer amazement after waiting and hoping so long for a child she thought she would never have. Elizabeth is old and had long since given up hope of having a child. Her wonder at what is going on in her womb most likely brought excitement and celebration.

Mary's awe is perhaps different. Her awe is fear and anxiety. Her awe is the result of a pregnancy that has come too soon. She is young, unmarried, and never could have imagined being "great with child," seeing as how she had never been with a man.

Elizabeth and Mary—both in awe as they ponder with expectation and trepidation what is gestating inside of them. And the amazing word from the scriptures is that God is the prime mover in what is happening inside them. Apart from God's activity in them, they would not be giving birth. Elizabeth was barren and menopausal. Mary was a virgin. God is giving birth to something in and through them.

Do not be confused. These stories in Luke 1 and 2 are about the miraculous activity of God, played out in the bodies of two ordinary human beings. Through the faithfulness of Dr. Luke, who has preserved these stories, we are given a window into the intersection of the human and the divine. In the case of Mary and Elizabeth, we are allowed to eavesdrop on their spiritual listening to what God is doing in their lives.

Mary, in particular, is of note to us in the season of Advent because she is the one who carries in her womb the Savior of all creation. She is the one in whom the Christ is gestating. And it is her, in particular, whom we take note of on this fourth Sunday in Advent and consider the question for our spiritual listening: what does God wish to birth in us this year?

The theological word for what happens at Christmas is *incarnation*. God becomes enfleshed in a person. "The Word became flesh and dwelled among us," John wrote in his Gospel. The means through which God became flesh was the human womb. Deep inside a particular human being named Mary, God became wrapped in human flesh and was born into our world. That is incarnation! The great truth of Christmas is not that incarnation *happened*, but that it *happens!* God continues to be born anew in his creatures even today.

In a sermon entitled "Mothers of God?", Dr. Fred Anderson drew on the ancient designation of Mary as *theotokos,* the "bearer of God." Or as our Eastern Orthodox brothers and sisters call Mary, the "mother of God." Drawing on this ancient way of describing Mary, Anderson wrote:

> …the promise and blessing of being a bearer of God is not limited to Mary alone. Are we not pregnant with God's promise? Deep within us, the Son of the Most

> High, the Savior of the World is coming into being, seeking to come to birth in you and in me. This is the good news—God has chosen you to bear him into the world. God has chosen me to bear him into the world. [xi]

Is it possible that we are all Marys in our own right? Is it possible that deep inside of us, deep down in that place within us where things grow and develop and eventually come forth, that God is looking to be born?

I want to suggest to you that such is indeed the case. God, in Jesus Christ, is looking to become a continuing incarnation in our world in each and every one of us. The good news of our Christian faith is that…

> …the babe who was born in Bethlehem;
>
> …the man who walked the fields of Galilee and the streets of Jerusalem;

…who was crucified on Golgotha and laid in a borrowed grave is present this day in the risen Christ, and he is continually seeking those in whom he may be born anew in their lives so they might bear him forth into the world.

Listen, Christian, deep within your being and tell me if you do not hear him. Do you not feel him moving in that innermost place? Fredrick Buechner writes of Christmas, "Year after year, the ancient tale of what happened is told—raw, preposterous, holy—and year after year the world in some measure stoops to listen."[xii]

Are you stopping to listen? Listen to the womb of your soul and tell me if you cannot hear Him. Of course, it will require an openness to listen and to relinquish your life. It did for Mary, and it will for us.

Mary received a visit from the angel Gabriel, who told her that she would bear a child. She had been chosen by grace to bear forth God's own Son into this world. And Mary responded with a question: "How can this be, since I am a virgin?"

Mary's question is not one of unbelief, but of openness, because whenever we are curious about the workings of God in our lives, we open ourselves to God. Mary was open—open to the possibilities of God that are beyond rational understanding. Gabriel responded by saying that she would be "overshadowed by the Most High." Through her openness to trust what she did not understand and her willingness to let her life be overshadowed by God, Christ was born into this world.

Perhaps, like me, you have always assumed that Mary had no choice in this matter. But that is not so. Mary responds to Gabriel by saying, “Let it be so! Let it be with me according to your word.”

Mary chooses the good news that Gabriel offers. She is a free moral agent in this process. She is open to what God is doing inside her womb, and she relinquishes her life to that Most High God who is working in the most intimate places of her being.

Mary said yes to God! The word to us in this Advent season is that if the incarnation is to continue to happen in our lives and world today, it will require our yes as well. We, just like Mary, must be open to the mysterious movement of God within us and be willing to let go of our lives.

What Mary opened herself to in this process sounds so spiritual and wonderful. But the reality is, it was quite mundane and, at times, very difficult. The same will be true for you and me if Christ is to be born in us.

For Mary, the journey she embraced that day brought with it all the challenges of a typical pregnancy—morning sickness and discomfort; swelling and skin problems; and perhaps postpartum depression. It meant becoming a refugee in Egypt. It meant raising a child through the terrible two’s and the angst of adolescence. It meant letting go when Jesus became an adult, and it meant risking what every parent fears most—losing your child to death.

Let us not be mistaken. If we open the deepest part of ourselves for Christ to be born in us, it does not mean that all will be sweetness and light. It means facing life in a real world. If Christ is to be born in us, it will not insulate us from the harsh realities of life in this world. It did not for Mary. It will not for us.

- It may mean going into places we’d rather not go, like bug-infested shacks to deliver Christmas food.
- It may mean approaching people we’d rather not approach: the homeless, the smelly, the dirty, and the crude.
- It may mean using our gifts of money and time and talent in a way that doesn’t just feather our own nest, but cares for the “least of these, Christ’s brothers and sisters.”

As Kathleen Norris writes, “Incarnation is the place…where hope contends with fear.”[xiii]

But listen to the good news. If we open our wombs—the most intimate part of ourselves so Christ may be born in us and borne by us—our lives will sing a new song.

Upon her visit to Elizabeth, Mary realized that all Gabriel had said to her was the truth. And in response, she sang. We call it "The Magnificat," based on the first words of the song in the Latin text.

"My soul magnifies the Lord."

Mary sings of:

- A time when all that opposes God's good purposes will be thwarted.
- A time when the lowly will be lifted up and the proud will be humbled.
- A time when the hungry will be filled and those who are full of themselves will be made to see their true emptiness.
- A time when the weak will have strength and the powerful will have mercy.

Mary sings of all these things as though they were already accomplished. All of Mary's verbs are in the past tense. She sings about a time to come as if it were already past. She, as Barbara Brown Taylor says, "Sings ahead of time," about what God will do.[xiv]

The good news for us this Christmas is that if Christ is born in us today, our lives, too, will sing a new song.

- In the face of disappointment and difficulty that life can bring, we will sing of victory and hope.
- In the wake of terrorism and fear, we will sing of peace and serenity.
- Despite the reality of death and pain, we will sing of life and healing.
- Regardless of the realities of life in this world, we will sing of a new world being born.

We will not only sing of that world; we will live as though it is already here.

In her book *Amazing Grace*, Kathleen Norris writes:

> There is a virgin place in our souls, a *point viege* as Thomas Merton calls it. It is a point untouched by illusion, a point of pure truth, which belongs entirely to God, inaccessible to the fantasies of our own mind or the brutalities of our own will. It is the Holy Spirit conceiving within us the pure possibility...of our lives.[xv]

Listen to the womb today, to the pure possibility of your life. May Christ be born in you, that your life may sing a new song. Amen.

Chapter 5

When Christmas Falls on Sunday

Christmas Day
2005

In those days a decree went out from Emperor Augustus that all the world should be registered. This was the first registration and was taken while Quirinius was governor of Syria. All went to their own towns to be registered. Joseph also went from the town of Nazareth in Galilee to Judea, to the city of David called Bethlehem, because he was descended from the house and family of David. He went to be registered with Mary, to whom he was engaged and who was expecting a child. While they were there, the time came for her to deliver her child. And she gave birth to her firstborn son and wrapped him in bands of cloth, and laid him in a manger, because there was no place for them in the inn.

In that region there were shepherds living in the fields, keeping watch over their flock by night. Then an angel of the Lord stood before them, and the glory of the Lord shone around them, and they were terrified. But the angel said to them, "Do not be afraid; for see—I am bringing you good news of great joy for all the people: to you is born this day in the city of David a Savior, who is the Messiah, the Lord. This will be a sign for you: you will find a child wrapped in bands of cloth and lying in a manger." And suddenly there was with the angel a multitude of the heavenly host, praising God and saying, "Glory to God in the highest heaven, and on earth peace among those whom he favors!" When the

> angels had left them and gone into heaven, the shepherds said to one another, "Let us go now to Bethlehem and see this thing that has taken place, which the Lord has made known to us." So they went with haste and found Mary and Joseph, and the child lying in the manger. When they saw this, they made known what had been told them about this child; and all who heard it were amazed at what the shepherds told them. But Mary treasured all these words and pondered them in her heart. The shepherds returned, glorifying and praising God for all they had heard and seen, as it had been told them (Luke 2:1–20).

Welcome to Christmas Sunday! This is the day when we celebrate the Nativity of our Lord. It feels good to be here in church today. Or does it? There's been quite a bit of controversy among church people in our country this year about whether to hold services on Christmas Day. Some churches have chosen not to have worship services today, among them some of the larger mega churches in our country, like the twenty-thousand-member Willow Creek Church just outside Chicago. In our own vicinity, First Baptist of Atlanta and North Point Church in Alpharetta have declined to hold services today.

It has been stated by some of these churches that Christmas Day is a "family time." In response, one could ask, is there a better thing for families to do on this day than to be in church and worship together?

But in fairness to many of these churches that have taken flak from their brothers and sisters, most of them held Christmas Eve services, as we did last evening. Some of those services were even midnight services, so technically those congregations did worship on Christmas Day. We Christians, myself included, are sometimes too quick to judge our brothers and sisters in the faith. In the process, we make ourselves feel superior, but we do not honor the Child who was born in lowliness and humility.

But this is the day when we celebrate the Nativity of our Lord. It feels good to be here today. Or does it?

I will confess to you that preachers and their families feel torn when Christmas falls on Sunday. We, just like you, have our family Christmas traditions. When Christmas falls on Sunday, those have to take a back seat.

I was reflecting this week on my years in the ministry when Christmas fell on Sunday. The last time was 1994. I did not preach on that Sunday, but we were in church at Peachtree Presbyterian in Atlanta. The evening before, on Christmas Eve, we had six worship services at the church. Cantey and I had responsibility for the 9 PM service, which was called "An Appalachian Christmas." Cantey formed and directed a choir just for that service. The choir sang old shaped-note Christmas music. We had a Bluegrass band and a storyteller, and we brought ten twenty-foot Douglas firs into the sanctuary to make it feel like a forest. We set all this up after the traditional candlelight service at 7 o'clock and had to take it all down and clean up before the 11 o'clock candlelight service that was televised nationally. I think we got home around midnight. And boy, was I glad I did not have to preach the next day. However, we did make it to church, where I think I may have dosed off during Dr. Harrington's sermon.

The year before that when Christmas fell on Sunday was 1988. I was pastoring in Chickamauga at that time. I preached that Sunday. In fact, this past week, I found a copy of that sermon in my files. It's written by hand. I did not have a computer, even though some were beginning to be available. That was a good Christmas season. Ashley had marched in the Chickamauga Christmas parade, twirling her baton with her other dance class members. She had also performed "A Chipmunk's Christmas" at the mall in Chattanooga. She was Alvin, the chipmunk.

Ian was only two years old on that Christmas, and he was only five feet tall and weighed 150 pounds! That was the Christmas when Ian decided to eat the glass Christmas tree ornaments. But as you see, he and we survived. That was the first time I experienced Christmas on a Sunday as a pastor. Needless to say, it was quite different. Our family Christmas traditions took a back seat.

When Christmas falls on Sunday, things are unsettling for Christians who make worship a priority on every Lord's Day. It feels different. But one thing that is not different is the story. The story of our Lord's birth remains the same, whether Christmas falls on Sunday or on some other day of the week. We are beckoned by that ancient story to, as the hymn says, "Come and worship, come and worship, worship Christ, the newborn King." [xvi]

Yes, the story remains the same no matter the day on which Christmas falls. So what we do here this morning is really not much different from what we do on every Sunday and, yes, what we do on every Christmas. We are here to worship—to worship the One who was born to Mary and Joseph in a humble stable in Bethlehem, the One who—mystery of mysteries—is God in the flesh.

The story is told of a church member who was asked to read the Nativity story of Luke 2 at the Christmas morning service. As she stood to read, she began by saying, "Now stop me if you've heard this before..." [xvii]

We have indeed heard this narrative before. It is not new. However, it is news. And it is good news at that.

> To you is born this day in the city of David a Savior,
> who is the Messiah, the Lord.

It was announced by angels, heard by poor shepherds, pondered by Mary and Joseph, and one could preach a sermon on any of those aspects of this familiar story. But on this Christmas, which falls on Sunday, I would like to invite us consider one little part of this familiar story that may be especially pertinent to us today. It is mentioned in verses six and seven:

> While they were there, the time came for her to deliver her child. And she gave birth to her firstborn son and wrapped him in bands of cloth, and laid him in a manger, because there was no place for them in the inn.

"No place for them in the inn." In this year when Christmas falls on Sunday, perhaps today more than ever, we are invited to consider making room. Yes, it would be easy to stay away from church today. It would have been easy to not hold service this morning and declare it "family day." It would have been easy for the personnel committee of the Session to say, "You know, our church staff works hard all year. They ought not to have to work on Christmas Day." It would have perhaps been easier on us all not to be here this morning, but I am glad we are. I'm glad you are here because it signals that we are trying to make room in our lives for the birth of Christ.

One of the great spiritual writers of our time, Father Thomas Merton, once penned a sermon entitled "The Time of No Room." In his sermon, Merton wrote:

> We live in the time of no room...The time when everyone is obsessed with lack of time, lack of space, with saving time, conquering space, projecting into

> time and space the anguish produced within them by the technological furies of size, volume, quantity, speed, number, price, power and acceleration.

If nothing else this morning, we are here in this hour of worship saying that we want to make room in our hearts and lives. We want to drop our obsession with lack of time and space, to drop all of our fretting and to make room. Isn't it true that we make room for that which is a priority? Our presence in worship this morning is a statement that worshipping the newborn King is a priority we desire in our lives. In this year when Christmas falls on Sunday, I would simply invite us to consider making room for Christ to be born anew in our lives—not letting any of our family traditions or personal desires push Christ away so he has to be born elsewhere than in the inn of our hearts.

In other words, this is an invitation to spiritual hospitality. It is an invitation to allow a space and time for Christ in our lives in this world where we are so often busy with one thing or another.

As I have done often in this Advent and Christmas season, I'd like to leave you with a story. There was once a Christmas pageant at a small church in which the part of the innkeeper at Bethlehem was played by a high school boy for whom the word "awkward" was an apt description—awkward in manner, awkward in social relationships, even awkward in size. His growing frame was always pushing the limits of his clothing. His peers liked him well enough, but he was the sort of person who was easy to overlook, to exclude from the center of things. When Joseph and Mary appeared at the inn, he stood—awkwardly—in the doorway, slumping a bit toward the couple as they made their request for lodging. He the dutifully recited his one line, "There is no room in the inn." But as Mary and Joseph turned and walked wearily away toward the cattle stall where they would spend the night, the boy continued to watch them with eyes filled with compassion. Suddenly responding to a grace which, though not a part of the script, filled the moment, he startled himself, the holy couple, and the audience by calling out, "Wait a minute. Don't go. You can have my room." [xviii]

When Christmas falls on Sunday, this is what Christ most wants to hear from us: "Wait a minute. Don't go. You can have my room!" May the room you have made for the birth of Christ this day allow you enjoy this Christmas as you have no other.

Chapter 6

Why Are You Searching for Me?

First Sunday after Christmas
2003

> Now every year his parents went to Jerusalem for the festival of the Passover. And when he was twelve years old, they went up as usual for the festival. When the festival was ended and they started to return, the boy Jesus stayed behind in Jerusalem, but his parents did not know it. Assuming that he was in the group of travelers, they went a day's journey. Then they started to look for him among their relatives and friends. When they did not find him, they returned to Jerusalem to search for him. After three days they found him in the temple, sitting among the teachers, listening to them and asking them questions. And all who heard him were amazed at his understanding and his answers. When his parents saw him they were astonished; and his mother said to him, "Child, why have you treated us like this? Look, your father and I have been searching for you in great anxiety." He said to them, "Why were you searching for me? Did you not know that I must be in my Father's house?" But they did not understand what he said to them. Then he went down with them and came to Nazareth, and was obedient to them. His mother treasured all these things in her heart. And Jesus increased in wisdom and in years, and in divine and human favor (Luke 2:41–52).

Christmas Day is past, but we still dwell in the season of Christmas. Yes, that's right. Christmas is indeed a season in the church, a period of twelve days, which usually includes two Sundays.

That is the reason we have sung some carols even today. In the stores, you will find that the Christmas décor has been taken down, and now Valentine's Day—what I call the most gauche holiday of the year (who would ever think of putting pink and red together?)—comes to the forefront. However, in the church, we linger with the mystery of the incarnation a little longer.

However, in the assigned gospel reading for the first Sunday after Christmas, we do not linger at the manger. No, we move forward twelve years. We move on to what is the only recorded story in the Bible about Jesus' boyhood. The story serves as an important bridge (in fact the only bridge) from the infant Jesus to the man Jesus.

The story contains layers of meaning and much fodder for those who would interpret it. There is any number of things one could focus on by way of sermon in this text. It is rich in meaning and message. For our purposes today, I'd like to call your attention to the first words of Jesus that are recorded by Luke in his Gospel. They take the form of a question, and the question is this: "Why are you searching for me?"

Of course, we need to know the context in which Jesus asks this question. Context is always pertinent to faithful biblical interpretation; otherwise, we find ourselves following the rabbit trails of our own bias and agendas. The context in which Jesus asks this question is in dialogue with his parents, Mary and Joseph, who had lost track of him in the midst of a Passover pilgrimage they had made to Jerusalem.

Jerusalem was a four-day journey south of Nazareth. The text tells us that Jesus and his family had the yearly tradition of making the trek to Jerusalem to celebrate the Passover. They most likely traveled in caravan with many friends and neighbors. It was a safer and easier way to travel in those days.

After worshipping at the Temple, Mary and Joseph loaded everything in the Rambler and headed home. Jesus wasn't in the back of the station wagon, but they were certain he must have been with some of the other parents in their caravan. However, a day into the trip, they suddenly realized that Jesus was nowhere to be found. In a state of panic, Joseph and Mary headed back to the Holy City. If you've ever gotten separated from your child, you can understand what must have been going through Mary and Joseph's minds.

After searching and searching, Mary and Joseph finally discover their son in the Temple with the teachers of the law. He is calmly sitting among them listening and asking questions. Mary and Joseph, as anxious parents do so often, express both relief and anger at their son. At this point, we read the first words from Jesus' lips in Luke's Gospel: "Why are you searching for me?"(Luke 2:48)

Let's reflect on the dimensions of meaning in Jesus' question to his parents. His question comes to us, as well, for is it not the case that we, too, search for Jesus? The better part of the Christian life as we know it in our time is a search for Jesus. In the last two centuries alone, there have been numerous searches for the true Jesus. The search for the historical Jesus, initiated in the nineteenth century by Albert Schweitzer, has continued to this day; the latest scholarly attempt is being called the Jesus Project, which is an effort to try to distill down as best as humanly possible the authentic and original Jesus from the biblical canon. Indeed, Jesus' question—"Why are you searching for me?"—is still relevant even today.

But it is not just a question for scholars. It is a question for every ordinary person who has ever encountered the One from Nazareth. And maybe the answer for us to Jesus' question is in keeping with the answer that Joseph and Mary would have made.

- Maybe, just like Joseph and Mary, we lost track of Jesus somewhere along the way.
- Maybe we got busy with other things.
- Maybe the journey involved taking care of so many details.
- Maybe we were so enjoying the scenery along the way that we never stopped to think that we had gotten separated from Him.
- Maybe we were neglectful and forgot about Him (some have suggested that Joseph and Mary in this passage are "bad parents;" who would ever forget about their child?).
- Maybe we took for granted that Jesus was there and never stopped to talk to Him, call out to Him, to see if He was there.

For whatever reason, sometimes we, just like Joseph and Mary, lose track of the precious Son in our lives.

And then, just like Jesus' parents, when we lose track of His presence, we perhaps lose faith in the sovereign power of God, and we become anxious, confused, frustrated, and angry.

When Mary and Joseph realized Jesus wasn't with them on their journey home, they went looking for him. Just like any good parents who love their child, they were anxious. They even admitted it when they finally caught up with their son. Mary said to Jesus, "Child, why have you treated us like this? Look, your father and I have been searching for you in great anxiety!" (v.48)

Eugene Peterson's translation of this verse in *The Message* helps us hear the anxiety of these parents who have lost their son: "Young man, why have you done this to us? Your father and I have been half out of our minds looking for you!"

Can you not hear the complex mixture of bewilderment, hurt, anger, and relief in Mary's words? And can we not also, if we listen to our own hearts, hear our own anxiety in our search for Jesus?

"Why have you treated us like this, Jesus?" That's what we ask in the midst of our confusion and pain when Jesus' presence is not plainly evident in our lives.

- When we are longing for meaning and purpose in our lives.
- When we wonder why things are the way they are in the world: hunger, pain, suffering and death, war and hatred.
- When we cannot find the answers we long for.

We cry out to Jesus: "Where are you? We have been searching everywhere for you! Why are you treating us like this? Can't you see how anxious and worried we are?"

And Jesus asks us, "Why are you searching for me?" He was right there all along, right where He was supposed to be! He was in His Father's house, going about His Father's business.

You get the impression from Jesus' response to Mary and Joseph that He wondered what the big deal was and what the search was all about. "Didn't you know that I must be in my Father's house?" (v. 49b)

Jesus was right there in the Temple, meeting with the teachers, listening to them, learning from them, talking with them. What we see in the whole story of Jesus and the Christian church is the consistent interplay of the Temple, the religious community, in the shaping of who He was and what His church would be.

It is in the Temple that Jesus is consecrated on the eighth day; the only boyhood record we have of Him is in the Temple; it is in the synagogue that Jesus reads from Isaiah and lays out His calling; it is in and around the Temple that Jesus has His give-and-take with the religious leaders of his day that forged his message of the Kingdom of God. It was in his community of faith that Jesus was found by Mary and Joseph that day. And the question for us may be, will we not indeed find the One we are searching for in the same place that His parents did—in the community of faith, the church?

We search far and wide for Jesus. We "wonder as we wander out under the sky;" we travel from here to there and delve into every imaginable esoteric subject to find Him. And all the while, He is in the Temple—in the community of faith—asking, "Why are you searching for me? Did you not know that I must be in my Father's house?"

In our searching for Jesus, I think we'd like a sexier answer. I think we'd like to have something a little more alluring than the answer that Jesus is found in the community of faith, "wherever two of three are gathered in His name." But there is no answer that is any better.

"Oh, the church is a mess!" we say. "I don't want anything to do with it anymore," I have heard people say. It's too conservative, say some. It's too liberal, say others. We have had people pull back from being in our midst here at FPC for both of those reasons. But by faith, we continue to gather in this imperfect institution called the "church" because Jesus has said that He must be here. We can search far and wide if we like, but the good news is that the One we are searching for has condescended to be among us in this crazy family we call the church:

- This place where we baptize our children and confirm them in the faith;
- This place where we try to do justice, show love and kindness, and walk humbly with our God;
- This place where we ask questions and try to learn from one another;
- This place where we break bread and pour wine;
- This place where we pray with and for one another;
- This place with so many warts and blemishes, but that is still the body of Christ.

"I must be in my Father's house." It's necessary that I be here, Jesus said. And if Jesus said that, is it any less necessary for us who are searching for this One who is the way, the truth, and the life?

After Christmas, we are often left with this empty feeling and wondering "what now?' The answer in our text today is, "We must be in our Father's house." Or, as another translation of that statement reads, we "must be about our Father's business." And so here's the answer to "What now, now that Christmas is over?"—Be in the community of faith and take that community with you into the world as you go about the Father's business of peace, justice, faith, hope, and love. For it is in our Father's house and going about our Father's business that we will discover the Jesus we are searching for.

Chapter 7

Living as Though Jesus Is Present

First Sunday after Christmas
2006

When the Son of Man comes in his glory, and all the angels with him, then he will sit on the throne of his glory. All the nations will be gathered before him, and he will separate people one from another as a shepherd separates the sheep from the goats, and he will put the sheep at his right hand and the goats at the left. Then the king will say to those at his right hand, "Come, you that are blessed by my Father, inherit the kingdom prepared for you from the foundation of the world; for I was hungry and you gave me food, I was thirsty and you gave me something to drink, I was a stranger and you welcomed me, I was naked and you gave me clothing, I was sick and you took care of me, I was in prison and you visited me." Then the righteous will answer him, "Lord, when was it that we saw you hungry and gave you food, or thirsty and gave you something to drink? And when was it that we saw you a stranger and welcomed you, or naked and gave you clothing? And when was it that we saw you sick or in prison and visited you?" And the king will answer them, "Truly I tell you, just as you did it to one of the least of these who are members of my family, you did it to me." Then he will say to those at his left hand, "You that are accursed, depart from me into the eternal fire prepared for the devil and his angels; for I was hungry and you gave me no food, I was thirsty and you gave

> me nothing to drink, I was a stranger and you did not welcome me, naked and you did not give me clothing, sick and in prison and you did not visit me." Then they also will answer, "Lord, when was it that we saw you hungry or thirsty or a stranger or naked or sick or in prison, and did not take care of you?" Then he will answer them, "Truly I tell you, just as you did not do it to one of the least of these, you did not do it to me." And these will go away into eternal punishment, but the righteous into eternal life (Matthew 25: 31–46) .

We have moved from the season of Advent to the season of Christmas. Advent is lived in anticipation and expectation of God coming to be with us in Christ. Christmas, on the other hand, is lived in celebration of Christ's arrival. As we sang on Christmas Eve:

Joy to the world, the Lord is come!

Let earth receive her King

As Christians, we believe that at Christmas we have indeed received the King among us. The child born in Bethlehem to the Virgin Mary is the One we worship and adore, the long-expected King of glory. His arrival in our world and our lives makes all the difference.

Or does it? Does the arrival of the Christ child and his continuing presence among us in the crucified and risen Jesus make a difference in our lives? It's a question I invite us to ponder this morning.

At least in the short-term, the answer to that question is probably yes. The birth of our Lord does make a difference in how we live, at least this time of the year. People are more generous in December, perhaps kinder, more genial, and civil. But what happens in January when all the decorations and lights are taken down and put away? What happens when school starts again or we return to the office? Do we continue to live like Jesus is here, like the King is among us?

The first Sunday after Christmas is a good time to consider these questions, especially because it falls on New Year's Eve this year and we stand ready to move into a fresh year.

The gospel text from Matthew we have read this morning is the lectionary text for New Year's Day. I found it an intriguing selection. What does the parable of the sheep and the goats (or as some have called it, the parable of the Last Judgment) have to say to us on the edge of a new year? As I pondered that, some clarity began to dawn.

New Year's Day is always in the season of Christmas. It always comes when we are acknowledging the presence of God among us in Jesus Christ. This parable is about the full and final presence of Christ among us at the end of time, when, as verse thirty-one says, "When the Son of Man comes in his glory, and all the angels with him, then he will sit on the throne of his glory."

Between Christ's first appearance at his Nativity and his final appearance at the Last Judgment—between the humble manger and the glorious throne—is where we are living. It seems from the overall witness of the New Testament that the challenge of the Christian life in this "between times" is to live each moment as though Jesus is present now. The question is, how do we do that? How do we live as though Jesus is here among us now?

I believe this text suggests two crucial spiritual movements for us as we stand on the brink of a new year in this Christmas season. The first spiritual movement is...

...To live with a view toward the eternal

We live in a culture of immediacy, locked into what Old Testament scholar and theologian Walter Bruggemann calls "the eternal present."[xix] All that matters for so many of us is today, this moment. We do not have a perspective toward eternity.

It plays itself out in our culture in a variety of ways: in the driving need for immediate gratification; in the buy-now-pay-later philosophy that puts us so in debt about this time each year; in the fact that so many of us have little or no savings to fall back on. As a society, we have little or no view toward the long term and certainly not toward eternity.

Therefore when we hear parables like this one of the final judgment, we find it difficult to imagine that there will ever be a time when we will be held accountable. We cannot seem to envision a time when we will be judged. We, in fact, resist the idea of a biblical judgment, forgetting that it is indeed a major component of both the Bible and the church's heritage.

Every week, you and I affirm in The Apostle's Creed that we believe in Jesus Christ with these words:

> He ascended in to heaven and sitteth on the right hand of God the Father Almighty. From thence he shall come to judge the quick and the dead.

From the right hand of the Father, Jesus shall come to judge the living (that's what is meant by that phrase "the quick") and the dead. We profess it. But we sometimes forget it is a tenant of our faith.

Jesus is our Savior, we profess.
Jesus is our Redeemer.
Jesus is our Friend.
But Jesus is also our Judge.

He is the one to whom we will be accountable at the end of history. It is not a welcome image in this culture of immediacy and non-judgementalism. However, it is a biblical one we must reckon with.

How would we live if we had a view toward eternity? How would we live if the Jesus we know as our Savior and Redeemer were also acknowledged to be the one who will judge us? I suspect we would live differently. We might find ourselves living as though Jesus is right here with us now.

In the National Cathedral, there is a gift shop, like there is in many big churches. And in that gift shop there is a sign posted to deter shoplifters that says, "We may not have seen you take it, but God did."

How would we live if we had the perspective of eternity, if we truly believed Jesus is watching us? I suspect we would live differently.

As we go forward into this new year, let us go forth with a view toward the eternal, living as though what we do right now has lasting consequences.

Yes, one spiritual movement for the New Year is to live with a view toward eternal. But a second spiritual movement goes hand in hand with the first and it is…

…To live with our eyes open toward the earthly

I grew up in a church tradition that spoke a great deal about the Last Judgment. You'd hear it almost every Sunday. "Get your heart right with Jesus, or you may end up being one of the goats that gets sent to hell." Hellfire and damnation was a regular message, and it often resulted in people coming forward down the aisle to "give their lives to the Lord."

But being an observant young man, I noticed that while people in my church talked a lot about eternity and made regular trips down the aisle, very little changed in some of their earthly lives. Some of them would still talk about the preacher behind his back. Some of them would continue to beat their children or wives. Some of them continued in their racist ways. It seemed many looked so forward to heaven that they were no earthly good.

We cannot escape the truth of the scriptures that we are called to have a view toward the eternal. But it is interesting that as the Bible—in particular, this parable—beckons us toward an eternal viewpoint, it does so by encouraging us to open our eyes toward the earthly.

Read the parable closely, and you will notice that the criteria for the Lord's division of the sheep from the goats in the world to come has a distinctly, this-world character. What is done in *this life* determines the Lord's disposition toward us in the life to come.

If we are to live as though Jesus is present here and now, then the parable tells us we must look downward, not upward. We must look toward "the least of these, our brothers and sisters." That is where heaven and earth converge—in the needful one before us.

Living as though Jesus is present is to live as though all of eternity depends on what we did on this earth, especially toward the one who is in need, because, as the parable states so clearly, Jesus is present in the needful one before us!

> If you did it to the least of these, you did it to me. (Matthew 25:40)

I once saw a T-shirt that said, "Please, God, don't let me be behind Mother Teresa at Judgment Day." I suppose that would be the prayer of each one of us. Few of us come close to being saints in caring for the least, the last, and the lost, but we can learn from those saints.

Mother Teresa once asked some visitors to her orphanage to hold up one hand and she said this:

> "The gospel is written on your fingers." Holding up one finger at a time, she accented each word: "You. Did. It. To. Me." Mother Teresa then added, "At the end of your life, your five fingers will either excuse you or accuse you of doing it unto the least of these. You did it to me." [xx]

Now lest we think Mother Teresa was challenging us all to leave our homes and go to Calcutta and care for orphans and untouchables, let me tell you what else she once said. During a visit to the United Nations, she said that not everyone is called to a ministry like hers. She said that day, "The greatest poverty among us is loneliness."

She said to parents, "Your calling is to love your children." She said to adult children, "Your calling is to love your aging parents."

Caring for "the least of these" involves opening our eyes to the earthly ones right in front of us. For, as the parable so clearly states, in them, Christ is to be found.

Dawn Mayes gave me a book for Christmas that I am enjoying reading: Barbara Brown Taylor's memoir of faith entitled *Leaving Church*. Reflecting on conflict with her congregation over what the Bible says, she wrote this:

> The whole purpose of the Bible, it seems to me, is to convince people to set the written word down in order to become living words in the world for God's sake. For me, this willing conversion of ink back to blood is the full substance of faith.[xxi]

We affirm at Christmas that the eternal Word of God that existed before time became flesh in the child born in Bethlehem. The calling for Christmas people is to take the Word that became flesh, that Word that is communicated to us in the ink on the pages of scripture, and allow it to become fleshed out once again in us where people are hurting and in need. For that is where Jesus continues to live today—in the "least of these."

Let us live the full substance of faith. Let us live like Jesus is present.

Endnotes

---

i Leonard Sweet, " "Return of the King" *Homiletics* Volume 15, Number 6 (November–December 2003): 45f.

ii Walter Wink, "Apocalypse Now?", found at www.religion-online.org, first printed in *The Christian Century* October 17, 2001 pp.16–19.

iii Father Gerry Pierse, *Gospel Reflections, found at www.bibleclaret.org.*

iv Sweet, "Return of the King" 44

v. Edward K. Rowell, ed., *Humor for Preaching and Teaching.* (Grand Rapids, Baker Books, 1996), 38.

vi Richard E. Van Harn, ed., *The Lectionary Commentary: The Third Readings—The Gospels.* (Grand Rapids, William B. Eerdmans, 2001), 308–309.

vii Author Unknown, "Crying in the Wilderness," *LectionAid* 12, no.1 (December 2003 – February, 2004): 3.

viii William Willamon, "Yearning for Christmas" *Pulpit Resource* No.4, Vol. 31 (October–December 2003): 42.

ix Willamon, "Yearning For Christmas," p.47.

x Julie Johnson, " "*Journeyers: Fostering a Christian Spirituality" CTS Vantage* (Fall/Winter 2003): 1.

xi Dr. Fred Anderson, sermon at Madison Avenue Presbyterian Church, New York, NY December 21, 1997.

xii Fredrick Buechner, *A Room Called Remember* (San Francisco, Harper & Row,1984), 61.

xiii Kathleen Norris, *Amazing Grace: A Vocabulary of Faith* (New York, Riverhead Books, 1998), 74–75.

xiv Barbara Brown Taylor, Home By Another Way, (Cambridge, Cowley Publications, 1999), 15

xv Kathleen Norris, *Amazing Grace: A Vocabulary of Faith* (New York, Riverhead Books, 1998), 74–75.

xvi Henry Thomas Smart, "Angels from the Realms of Glory."

xvii Alan Meyers, "Theological Themes" *Lectionary Homiletics*, Number 1, Volume XVII (December 2005–January 2006): 32.

xviii Dr. Thomas Long, "Shepherds and Bathrobes" in *Something Is About to Happen…* (Lima, Ohio, CSS Publishing, 1987), 45.

xix Walter Bruggemann, *Prophetic Imagination* (Philadelphia, Fortress Press, 1978) 28f.

xx Dr. Hal Brady, sermon at First United Methodist Church, Dallas, Texas, October 11, 1992.

xxi Barbara Brown Taylor, *Leaving Church: A Memoir of Faith* (San Francisco, Harper Collins, 2007), 107.